"How far that little candle throws his beams! So shines a good deed in a weary world."
—William Shakespeare, *The Merchant of Venice*

"I have no color prejudices nor caste prejudices nor creed prejudices. All I care to know is that a man is a human being, and that is enough for me." —Mark Twain

"Do your little bit of good where you are; it's those little bits of good put together that overwhelm the world."
—Desmond Tutu

"When I was young, my ambition was to be one of the people who made a difference in this world. My hope is to leave the world a little better for having been there."
—Jim Henson

"Be a rainbow in someone else's cloud." —Maya Angelou

"A single act of kindness throws out roots in all directions, and the roots spring up and make new trees."
—Amelia Earhart

"Let no one ever come to you without leaving better and happier." —Mother Teresa

Other books in the **When I Grow Up...**
children's book series by Wigu Publishing:

When I Grow Up I Want To Be...in the U.S. Army!
When I Grow Up I Want To Be...a Teacher!
When I Grow Up I Want To Be...a Firefighter!
When I Grow Up I Want To Be...in the U.S. Navy!
When I Grow Up I Want To Be...a Veterinarian!
When I Grow Up I Want To Be...a Nurse!
Cuando Crezca Quiero Ser...¡veterinaria!
Cuando Crezca Quiero Ser...¡soldado del Ejército de EE.UU.!

Look for these titles in the **When I Grow Up...**
children's book series soon:

When I Grow Up I Want To Be...a World Traveler!
When I Grow Up I Want To Be...a Race Car Driver!
When I Grow Up I Want To Be...a Police Officer!
When I Grow Up I Want To Be... Green!
When I Grow Up I Want To Be...a Rock Star!
When I Grow Up I Want To Be...in the U.S. Air Force!
When I Grow Up I Want To Be...an Astronaut!
When I Grow Up I Want To Be...an Ocean Explorer!
When I Grow Up I Want To Be... Healthy!
When I Grow Up I Want To Be...a Park Ranger!

Please visit www.whenigrowupbooks.com for more information.
Please like us at www.facebook.com/whenigrowupbooksbywigu.

When I Grow Up® I Want To Be...

a Good Person!

Wigu Publishing | Sun Valley, ID

Library of Congress Control Number: 2015916206
ISBN 978-1-939973-04-7

The words **When I Grow Up...** is a registered trademark of Wigu Publishing, LLC.
The word **Wigu** and the **Wigu logo** are registered trademarks of Wigu Publishing, LLC.
The words **When I Grow Up I Want To Be...** and **Cuando Crezca Quiero Ser...** are registered trademarks of Wigu Publishing, LLC.

Wigu Publishing is a collaboration among talented and creative individuals working together to publish informative and fun books for our children. Our titles serve to introduce children to the people in their communities who serve others through their vocations. Wigu's books are unique in that they help our children to visualize the abundant opportunities that exist for them to be successful and to make a difference. Our goal is to inspire the great leaders and thinkers of tomorrow.

First edition, paperback, 2015

10 9 8 7 6 5 4 3 2 1

Quantity sales: Special discounts are available on quantity purchases by corporations, associations, promotional organizations, and others. For details, please contact the publisher at

Wigu Publishing
P.O. Box 1800
Sun Valley, ID 83353
inquiries@wigupublishing.com

Please visit our website at www.whenigrowupbooks.com for more information.

Proudly printed and bound in the United States of America.

When Brendan and Blake were young, their mother always read them their favorite story: "The Elephant and the Blind Men." It is a tale of learning, as all tales should be.

For Blake and Brendan,

going to a funeral seems

like a really bad idea.

But what they discover

might just change their

minds for good!

"I don't want to go to anyone's funeral," said Blake.

"Me neither," said Brendan.

"Mr. Becket was not just 'anyone,'"
said Dad.

OBITUARY NOTICE

Thomas "Tommy" Becket, age 88, passed away peacefully on June 16, surrounded by family and friends. Mr. Becket was known throughout our hometown as a generous and kind man who tried to see good in everyone he met and left everyone who met him better for it. Mr. Becket will be remembered in our hearts as a good man. His wife of 58 years, Karen Rose, his three sons, seven grandchildren, and four great-grandchildren survive Mr. Becket.

Services to be held at Canterbury Church, 111 Park Avenue, Saturday, June 20, 9 a.m. Reception to follow. All are welcome.

Loving husband of Brown; beloved fat Brown, Kathy and (and devoted longti of Betty Gusdorf; cl father of Christophe Smith, Stephen (M and Melissa Baer; a great-grandchildren sured caregiver Mer neral service will be day, October 7, 10 a.t Chapel, 1170 Rockv terment King Dav Gardens. Family will Shiva on Wednesday residence of Kathy Smith. Memorial may be made to Osh Learning Institute at

"Do we have to go? Can't we just stay home? I'm tired," said Brendan.

"Me, too," said Blake. "I want to watch TV."

"I'm tired of discussing it with you," said Dad. "You two are going. That's the end of it."

"But, why do we have to go?" asked Blake.

"Yeah, why?" repeated Brendan.

"Because it's the right thing to do," answered Dad. "Mr. Becket was a good man who was kind and generous to everyone in town, including us. We are going to pay our respects to his family, to his memory."

"Do we really have to go, Mom?" asked Brendan.

"Absolutely," answered Mom. "Listen to your Dad. And hurry up. I don't want to be late."

There might be ghosts. I don't want to see any ghosts, thought Brendan.

"Sometimes in life, we all have to do things we don't want to do but *should* do. This is one of those times," said Dad.

"He won't even know we are there!" said Blake.

Unless he's a ghost, thought Brendan.

"I will know. Your mom will know. And most importantly, his family will know," said Dad firmly.

"Boys, we are going to Mr. Becket's funeral because he set a good example of how to live, how to be a good person," said Mom. "Now, get ready, please. I put your good clothes out on your beds. I won't ask again."

"Why do we have to get all dressed up?" asked Blake.

"What kind of question is that? Why do you think?" said Dad. "Of course you are going to get dressed up—out of respect. Everyone will be dressed up."

"Now, get a move on. I don't want to be late!" Mom said again.

Blake and Brendan got dressed. They even wore their clip-on ties.

"Is everyone ready to go? Finally?" asked Dad, holding the front door.

"Just combing the boys' hair," said Mom.

"That hurts, don't pull!" complained Brendan.

"Stop fidgeting so much, and it won't," said Mom. "Finally, you're done."

Finally! thought Brendan.

The family got in the car. It took 12 minutes to drive up to the church on Park Avenue, where the funeral service for Mr. Becket was to be held. Brendan counted every second and elbowed Blake for sitting too close.

Mom said, "Both of you, please, just behave yourselves. No fighting. Dad, do something, please."

"Boys, that's it! Don't make me stop the car!" yelled Dad impatiently.

Blake said, "It was Brendan's fault. Do we have to stay long?"

"We haven't even gotten there, and you're already asking that?" asked Dad.

"What's going to happen when we get there?" asked Blake.

"There will be a service first, and then there will be a reception afterwards. It will be a gathering for the family and friends to remember the good things about Mr. Becket. We mourn Mr. Becket's passing at the service. We celebrate his life at the reception."

Sounds gloomy and boring, thought Blake.

Sounds spooky and scary, thought Brendan. *I really hope there are no ghosts there.*

As they pulled up in front of the church, a sign read, "Parking Lot Full."

"I told you we were going to be late," said Mom.

"It's not my fault," said Blake.

"Me neither," said Brendan.

"We are not late," said Dad. "Everyone relax, please. I guess there are more people than they expected," he said, as he turned the car around. He found a place to park halfway down the street. So did a lot of other families.

Brendan and Blake saw some of their neighbors and a few of their school friends. They waved, but no one said much. Actually no one said anything until Blake asked, "Can I go in with my friend Carlos?"

"Me, too?" asked Brendan.

Blake elbowed Brendan. "Find your own friends."

"We will go in together as a family," said Dad.

Walking from the car to the church, the

family passed by Mr. and Mrs. Potts's house. Mr. Potts was sitting on his front porch.

"Hi, Mr. Potts. Are you going to Mr. Becket's funeral?" Brendan shouted across the front yard to Mr. Potts, a bit too loud. Mom cringed.

"No, afraid not. Not me," responded Mr. Potts. He always spoke in short sentences. "Suppose I should. Good guy. Mrs. Potts kept telling me I should. She went without me. Don't like going to funerals. Nope."

How come he gets to stay home? Blake asked himself.

As the family walked past Mr. Potts's house, Dad said, "Boys, some people, like Mr. Potts, have a difficult time with funerals, especially if it's for someone they really liked. We all do."

Just then, a thought came to Blake. *Mom and Dad might be having a hard time just like Mr. Potts. I thought being a grown-up meant*

you could do whatever you wanted, but maybe not.

Blake turned around and called out, "Mr. Potts, do you want to come with us? It would be ok."

Mr. Potts hesitated for a moment and then he shook his head. "Thanks. Don't think so. Thanks anyway."

No one said anything more as they walked up the street. Blake started counting the cracks on the sidewalk to himself. When he got to 117 cracks, they were in front of the church. *Finally.*

As the family walked up the steps to the church, they came upon a crowd of people. They were in a line waiting to write in a book on a table just past the front door.

"What's going on? What are they doing?" asked Blake.

Dad said, "They are signing the guest book to let Mr. Becket's family know who was here today. You can sign if you want. What do you think?"

Blake looked at Brendan. He shook his head.

"It's up to you," said Dad.

"It would be a nice thing to do," said Mom.

"Let's just go in," said Blake.

I wonder if the ghosts are hiding somewhere. I wonder if Mr. Becket's ghost is waiting behind the door, thought Brendan.

"A lot of people showed up," said Dad, as the family walked into the church.

"I wonder how many people will come to my funeral," said Blake. "I guess I'll find out."

"Who cares?" said Brendan. "You'll be dead so you won't even know."

"I might be a ghost, then I'll know," said Blake. "Anyway, no one will come to your funeral at all."

"Boys!" said Mom. "One more time and we

are going home."

I wish, thought Blake.

Just then a man in a dark suit, with pants that were a little too short, came to the stage at the front of the church. "Would everyone now please take their seats?" he asked.

"I don't want to sit in the front row," whispered Blake. "They might call on me."

Brendan snorted, "No one is going to call on you! This isn't school! And no one calls on you anyway!"

"Boys, please mind your manners," said Mom. The family found a bench to sit on halfway back.

Everyone got very quiet, and the man in the dark suit began speaking.

"Welcome, friends and relatives of Mr. Becket. We are here today to say good-bye to a dear, dear friend.

"Many of you know me as Pastor Jones,

but I am not here to preach today. I think if we all remember how Mr. Becket lived his wonderful life, that will be today's lesson.

"Some people go through life and never make a difference," he continued. "We all have choices to make about how we live our lives. Some people go through life and touch the lives of others. Mr. Becket was one of them. He made a difference in the lives of many of us. He did it by example and by helping others whenever and wherever he could."

I thought he said he wasn't going to preach, thought Blake.

"Mr. Becket saw the good in people that others could not. He planted seeds of ideas and hopes for each of us.

"Join us today as we celebrate his life and the joy, kindness, and generosity he brought to everyone he knew. Let us honor his memory by trying to be more like him."

Everyone seemed to nod in agreement. Then Pastor Jones said, "Now, our Mrs. Green would like to say a few words."

A woman in a black dress stepped up to the podium at the front of the church.

"Hello. My name is Elizabeth Green. It's so good to see so many nice people here this morning. I was one of Mr. Becket's many friends—for more than forty years. My house is the one on Elm Street with all of the flowers and plants all over."

"Her garden *is* pretty amazing," whispered Mom.

"You know, it was Mr. Becket who first gave me the idea to take up gardening after Mr. Green, my husband, passed away. At first, I could not even grow weeds. Well, actually, Mr. Becket said I was pretty good at that!"

A few people in the audience chuckled.

"At the time, I didn't even know that

Mr. Becket knew so much about gardening," she continued. "But, he showed me exactly what plants were best to grow at what time of year and just how to do it. He said we all had a responsibility to make the world a more beautiful place, each in our own way. He did, and he helped me do the same in my own way.

"I brought some flowers from my garden here today, and I hope you enjoy them just as much as I do. I guess it's my way of saying thank you to Mr. Becket. I think of him and thank him every time a new flower blooms."

"Isn't that nice?" said Mom.

Pastor Jones came up again and said, "Thank you, Mrs. Green. There is someone else who would like to say a few words."

"Mom, my butt hurts from this bench," said Blake.

Mom gave Blake "the look" but didn't say a word.

A man with gray hair in a gray suit stood at

the front now and started talking.

"Hello, everyone, and thank you for being here today. I'm sure it was as difficult for many of you as it was for me. Tommy Becket and I grew up together. He was one of my very best friends. We went to elementary school, middle school, and high school together," he said.

"One of the best things about Tommy was how he cared for other people and, in particular, for those who could not stand up for themselves. I want to tell you a story about a boy, Bob Bullford. Back in school, he was the class bully. All the kids called him Bob the Bully. Tommy always said bullies were cowards—that they really didn't have a problem with the kids they were picking on but had a problem with themselves.

"One day on the playground, Bob the Bully was picking on a bunch of little kids. Tommy went up to Bob the Bully and told him to stop it.

"Bob the Bully gave Tommy a shove. But Tommy punched Bob back and gave him a bloody nose. Bob had to go to the school nurse.

"Tommy got blamed by the school for picking the fight and was punished. But the school soon found out the truth and Bob got suspended for a week. His parents were really mad. I think he learned his lesson. He promised to be good and was allowed one more chance. He never bullied anyone ever again. Then, even more amazingly, Bob and Tommy became good friends. Now, I don't recommend for you young kids here today to go and punch anyone, but do stand up for those being bullied and go get help from a teacher or a trusted adult.

"It took a lot of courage for Tommy to stand up to Bob, but I tell this story not because Tommy saved all the other little kids from Bob the Bully, but because Tommy saved

Bob from himself.

"Thank you."

Pastor Jones came back up to the podium and said, "Thank you for those wonderful memories. Now, all of you are invited to join us in the reception room."

Slowly, everyone moved to a big room next door with a very high ceiling, stained glass windows, and a lot of beautiful flowers.

I wonder if those are from Mrs. Green's house, Brendan thought to himself.

As the family joined the crowd of people, Brendan said, "I see our old school nurse. Should we say hello or what?"

"Mom, can we go over and say hello to Mrs. Ellis?" Blake asked.

"Of course," said Mom. "Just be on your best behavior as always."

"Hello, Mrs. Ellis," said Brendan.

"Hello, Brendan. Hi, Blake," said Mrs. Ellis.

She was always nice, thought Blake.

"Mrs. Ellis, we haven't seen you for a while. There's a new nurse at school this year."

"Yes, it's good to see you again! How is that new nurse treating you?" she grinned.

Brendan shrugged. "She's alright."

"Are you still a nurse?" asked Brendan.

"Yes, of course," replied Mrs. Ellis. "But now I work at the hospital."

"Is the hospital better than the school?" asked Blake.

"It's not better, it's just different. We get patients of all ages, not just kids. Mr. Becket was one of our patients."

"Why did he die?" asked Blake. Then he felt embarrassed that he had asked.

"Sometimes people just die," said Mrs. Ellis. "Everyone does at some point. Mr. Becket was older, and he got very sick. It just caught up with him. I think he had a good life,

though. Eighty-eight years is a pretty long time."

Eighty-eight years seems like forever, thought Blake. "Did you see Mr. Becket at the hospital?"

Mrs. Ellis nodded. "Yes! I helped take care of him. He was a good patient. I think he knew he was dying, but he was very brave about it. We all tried to keep him comfortable. We tried to keep Mr. Becket cheered up, but I think he did more to cheer us up than we did for him. He was always telling us stories. Some were pretty funny. He had a lot of visitors, including your parents. Every time one of them left, Mr. Becket would tell us a story about them and just how he happened to know them. I see many of them are here today. He had a great life and a lot of great friends."

"Did he tell you any secret stuff about Mom and Dad?" asked Brendan.

"No. A person like Mr. Becket would never do that. Mr. Becket had a lot of good memories, and I think he left all of us with a lot of good memories, too. Maybe that's what we're all meant to do here on Earth—be a good person and create good memories for everyone," replied Mrs. Ellis. "Maybe that is more than enough. Maybe that's everything!"

She smiled. "Well, it was good seeing you again and seeing how much you two have grown up."

"Look!" Blake exclaimed. "There's Captain Kirby from the firehouse."

"Hi, Captain Kirby!" Brendan called out. "Do you remember us from the school field trip to your fire station?"

"Of course! Very sad about Mr. Becket, though. I guess you kids must have known him?" asked Captain Kirby.

"Sort of. He helped Dad fix the sink when it leaked out all over the kitchen floor," said

Blake. "Our parents told us we had to come to pay our respects."

"They were right. You know Mr. Becket helped a lot of people," said Captain Kirby.

"Fact is, I probably wouldn't even be a firefighter today if it weren't for Mr. Becket."

Brendan's eyes widened. "Really?"

"Oh man! I was always getting into trouble, and my parents didn't know what to do with me. I was kind of out of control. My father asked Mr. Becket to talk to me. Mr. Becket said I was just getting into trouble because I needed something to do. I had too much energy!" said Captain Kirby.

"Did you know Mr. Becket was a volunteer firefighter when he was younger?" continued the captain. "Well, he took me down to the fire station. The fire captain introduced me to all the people he worked with and showed me all around."

"Like you did for us!" said Blake.

"Exactly!" replied Captain Kirby. "I looked at the fire trucks and the gear and just dreamed of wearing a firefighter's uniform!"

"Now *you're* the fire captain!" said Brendan.

"Mr. Becket told me it was not a uniform that made people good or important. It came from inside—from wanting to help people in need. But the outfits are still pretty cool! So is being a firefighter and helping people in trouble instead of getting into trouble yourself. Helping others really helps you be a better person. That's what Mr. Becket always said. I guess that's why Mr. Becket was such a good person. He helped so many of us."

"I'd like to wear a firefighter's uniform someday," Blake said.

"A firefighter's uniform is like being a good person," said Captain Kirby. "Sometimes you have to grow into it."

The boys nodded.

"Anyway guys, be good! Have your dad

bring you by the station anytime—well, anytime we are not out on a call!"

As Captain Kirby left, Blake and Brendan were surprised to find their parents talking to Mr. Williams, their PE teacher from school.

Blake was first to greet him. "Hi, Mr. Williams. Did you know Mr. Becket, too?"

"Sure! He used to help out as an assistant coach for almost every sport I can think of."

"I thought he was a volunteer firefighter!" Brendan exclaimed.

"That, too! But Tom always wanted to be a baseball player for New York. He even made it to the minor leagues, but he got injured. That ended his dream of becoming a sports superstar. So he volunteered as a coach and taught us about sports and a whole lot more."

"A whole lot more? Like what?" asked Blake.

"Like that as much as I wanted to be a great

soccer player myself, I was not quite fast enough or strong enough," answered Mr. Williams. "Mr. Becket explained to me that if I could not be a professional soccer player, then maybe I could do something more important, like being a coach who could help kids become better kids, or even sports stars themselves."

"So, are you sad you were never a soccer star?" asked Brendan.

"No. Well, maybe a little at first. But now, not at all! Mr. Becket taught us that life is like one big, important game and that honesty, teamwork, fair play, respect for yourself and others, and following rules are important aspects of sports as well as life. So, PE is no different from math or history. The idea is to learn as much as you can, work hard, and play fair."

"Dad tells us that all the time," said Brendan. Dad smiled.

"I thought PE was just for exercise," said Blake.

"Do you know what PE stands for? It stands for Physical Education," responded Mr. Williams. "So it means both exercise and education. Mr. Becket taught us that the challenges we face in sports help us to develop confidence, self-esteem, and motivation in everything we do."

Sometimes I have trouble even getting up in the morning, thought Blake.

"He taught us how to deal with winning and losing and how to do both gracefully," continued Mr. Williams. "And, that being part of a team helps us learn how to get along with everyone, wherever we are."

I still hate losing, thought Brendan.

"So, thanks to Mr. Becket, I have been able to share the great lessons he taught me with hundreds of kids like you over the years and to help them improve their lives and make healthy choices. And I have to tell you, that makes me feel a whole lot better than being a professional soccer star, and it's much more rewarding," said Mr. Williams.

"More rewarding?" asked Blake. *Sports stars make lots of money,* he thought to himself.

"Yes. Rewarding in the ways that really matter," responded Mr. Williams.

"I still want to be a sports superstar," said Brendan.

"That's fine. Just be the best you can…in all things," said Mr. Williams. "That's what counts."

Blake and Brendan said good-bye to Mr. Williams and asked Dad, "Can we go home now, please?"

"Not quite yet, boys."

Brendan asked Mom, "Is it time to go home?"

"Brendan, your dad just told both of you, not yet."

Blake turned to Brendan and shrugged. "Guess that means not yet."

Brendan said to Blake, "Well, there's Dr. Helen, the animal doctor. Let's say hello to her."

Blake said, "She's called a veterinarian."

"Hi, guys! Good of you to come today," she said.

"I guess everyone knew Mr. Becket," said Brendan to Dr. Helen.

"I think he touched everyone's lives," said Dr. Helen.

"Did Mr. Becket have a pet?" asked Blake.

"Actually, he had a cat quite a few years ago. It was a stray he rescued from the animal shelter. The cat had been abused by its owners, so it behaved badly and didn't trust anyone. The shelter didn't think anyone would adopt him until Mr. Becket came around."

"What did he do?" asked Brendan.

"He understood that all the cat needed was someone who could be very patient and kind so that the cat would trust people again," said Dr. Helen, smiling. "He once told me that 'we can judge the heart of a person by the way they treat animals.' I will never forget that!"

"That was really nice of him," said Blake.

"Well, great to see you two boys," said Dr. Helen. "And remember to take care of all animals…they need you as much as you need them!"

A voice with a familiar accent called to them from behind. "Hello, boys!"

When Brendan and Blake turned around, they saw Mr. Patel. He owned the grocery store on Main Street that they passed on the way home from school each day. Whenever the boys went in, Mr. Patel gave them special twisted doughnuts called *imarti*. Free. Just to be nice.

Mr. Patel said he made them every day using his mother's recipe, which was famous

throughout all of western India. Mr. Patel had a lot of food that looked strange to Blake and Brendan but tasted delicious.

Blake always looked at the dollar bill Mr. Patel had framed and hanging on the wall behind the counter. The note on it read, "Our first dollar."

"Hello, Mr. Patel," Blake greeted him. "Did you know Mr. Becket? Was he a big customer? I used to see him in your store sometimes."

"A big friend. Not so much a big customer, but an important one, for sure!"

"How can you be important and not big?" asked Brendan.

"Friends are always important. You two are my friends," replied Mr. Patel.

The boys smiled.

"You know, when I opened my grocery store many years ago, Mr. Becket was my very first customer. Other people would not shop at my store. I thought maybe some people did not come in because of the way I looked or because I dressed differently. And my food was unfamiliar to most people way back then. I thought I might go broke!

"Mr. Becket came into my store and treated me just like any other person right from the start. Some people judge you by how you look or dress or the religion you practice, but not Mr. Becket. He was better than that. He loved my store and told everyone about it. Sooner than I had hoped, more and more people were coming in! I had a lot of good customers and good friends!"

"My dad really likes your bread," said Brendan.

"Yes," replied Mr. Patel. "Many people like *naan* bread. But if it weren't for Mr. Becket, many people in this town would never have discovered it, and I would not still be in business today."

And we wouldn't be getting free doughnuts, thought Blake.

"So Mr. Becket was your first customer?" Brendan asked.

"Yes, the first one to walk through my door to say welcome and to buy something," answered Mr. Patel.

"So that's his dollar on the wall in your store!" exclaimed Blake.

"It is indeed!" said Mr. Patel.

"When you look at it, do you think of how much money you made thanks to Mr. Becket?" asked Blake.

"Oh, maybe a little. But there is much more to it than that. It reminds me that friendships and understanding are worth more than all the money in the world."

Just then, Blake was surprised to see Mr. Potts talking with Pastor Jones at the reception.

Mr. Potts came over to greet the boys. "Yes, I know. Said I wasn't going. Thought to myself, 'If the boys can do it, so can I.' So here I am. I'm glad. So is Mrs. Potts. Thank you, boys."

"For what?" asked Blake.

"For showing me the right thing to do. Anyway. Thanks," said Mr. Potts.

Blake and Brendan just stared at each other.

The family was getting ready to leave when Dad stopped by to say hello to one more person. It was the man who told the Bob the Bully story.

"Everyone, meet Bob Bullford," said Dad.

"Wonderful meeting you all," said Bob Bullford, in a kind voice. Then he turned to Blake and Brendan, smiled, winked, and walked away.

Blake, totally surprised, turned to Dad and asked, "Bob Bullford? Was that Bob the Bully?"

"Not anymore. He only used to be," said Dad.

Wow, thought Blake. *He was telling the story about himself.*

"Wow," said Brendan.

Then Mom smiled and said, "You never know about some people. Well, I think it's time to go."

Finally, thought Blake.

Everyone liked Mr. Becket a lot. It all went pretty fast, thought Brendan. *And I didn't see any ghosts! I wonder if there really are such things.*

It really wasn't that bad, thought Blake. *I wonder if I can be as good a person as Mr. Becket when I grow up.*

As they left the church, Blake turned to Brendan and said, "Maybe we should sign the guest book."

Dad said, "That would be good of you."

Brendan nodded. "Yeah, I guess we should."

And they did.

"Dad," said Blake, "I want to be like Mr. Becket when I grow up. I want to be a good person to everyone."

"Me, too," said Brendan.

"I think you two are well on your way," said Dad.

"Maybe you two could start by being nicer to each other," Mom suggested.

Blake and Brendan looked at each other and at the same time said, "Nah!"

"Boys!" said Dad.

After a few seconds, both boys grinned and said, "Just kidding!"

Mom smiled and said, "Do you boys remember the story I used to read to you at bedtime about the elephant and the blind men? Well, like the elephant in the story, being a good person is not just one single thing but is the total of everything you do.

And like the elephant in the story, people won't forget it!"

"I loved that story," said Blake.

"Me, too," said Brendan. "Can you read it to us again tonight?"

"Of course," said Mom happily. And she did.

The Elephant and the Blind Men

Once upon a time, there lived six blind men in a village.

One day the villagers told them, "Hey, there is an elephant in the village today."

They had no idea what an elephant was because they had never seen one. They decided, "Even though we are not able to see it, let us go and feel it." All of them went to where the elephant was and every one of them touched it.

"The elephant is a pillar," said the first man, who touched his leg.

"Oh no! It is like a rope," said the second man, who touched the tail.

"Oh no! It is like a thick branch of a tree," said the third man, who touched the trunk of the elephant.

"It is like a big hand fan," said the fourth man, who touched the ear of the elephant.

"It is like a huge wall," said the fifth man, who touched the belly of the elephant.

"It is like a solid pipe," said the sixth man, who touched the tusk of the elephant.

They began to argue about the elephant, and each one of them insisted that he was right. It looked like they were getting angry.

A wise man was passing by. He saw them arguing. He stopped and asked, "What is the matter?"

They answered, "We cannot agree on what an elephant is."

Each one of them told what he thought the elephant was like. The wise man calmly explained to them, "All of you are right. The reason every one of you is telling it differently is that each one of you touched a different part of the elephant. Actually, the elephant has all those features you described."

The men were amazed. There was no more fight. They felt happy that they all were right.

Made in the USA
Charleston, SC
05 January 2016